ZANZIBAR AND KILIMANJARO TRAVEL GUIDE 2023: The Updated Guide to the Best Attractions: Discover the Breathtaking Beauty of Zanzibar Coast, Africa's Highest Mountain, Must see sights and Hidden gems in Tanzania, Pristine Beaches, Historical Stone Town, Vibrant Culture, Things to Do.

TABLE OF CONTENT

My Memorable Travel Experience
Inspiring future trips and adventures

Chapter 1: Introduction

Welcome to Zanzibar and Kilimanjaro

Welcome to the vibrant world of Zanzibar and Kilimanjaro! In this updated travel guide, we're thrilled to take you on an unforgettable journey through the breathtaking beauty of Tanzania's treasures. Whether you're an adventure enthusiast, a nature lover, or a culture seeker, this guide is your compass to discovering the hidden gems and must-see attractions that await you.

Imagine stepping into a world where sparkling blue waters meet golden sandy shores in Zanzibar. It's like walking into a dream where history comes alive in the charming Stone Town, and you'll taste yummy new foods that you've never tried before.

Zanzibar, with its pristine beaches and historical Stone Town, invites you to explore a coastal paradise where azure waters meet white sands. The island's vibrant culture and tantalizing cuisine promise an immersion into a tapestry of traditions and flavors.

Now, let's talk about Kilimanjaro – Africa's tallest mountain! Picture yourself on a big adventure, climbing higher and higher, passing through different kinds of forests, and seeing animals along the way. And guess what? When you reach the tip-top, you'll feel like a superhero, standing way above the clouds!

Kilimanjaro, Africa's highest mountain, stands as an awe-inspiring challenge for those seeking to conquer its majestic peak. As you ascend through diverse ecosystems, you'll witness nature's wonders unfold and experience a triumph of determination and perseverance.

Tanzania, rich in natural beauty, offers a plethora of adventures. From the famous Serengeti National Park's wildlife spectacle to the lesser-known treasures tucked away in its landscapes, this guide leads you on a captivating safari.

Get ready to soak up the sun on Zanzibar's beaches, embrace the rhythm of local music and dance, and embark on thrilling wildlife safaris. As you delve into this guide, you'll find practical tips, cultural insights, and a roadmap to curating your own extraordinary Tanzanian experience.

On this journey, you'll meet friendly people, listen to exciting music, and even learn some Swahili words to make new friends. Plus, we'll show you the best spots to see wild animals like lions, elephants, and zebras, just like in the movies!

So, pack your curiosity and spirit of exploration as we set forth on a journey through Zanzibar's coastal charm, Kilimanjaro's majestic heights, and Tanzania's captivating wonders. Let's discover the heart and soul of this enchanting East African destination together.

About this Travel Guide: Your Ultimate Companion to Zanzibar and Kilimanjaro Adventures

Hey dear traveler! I want to make sure you have the best journey ever, which is why I put together this special guide just for you. Here's what you need to know about it:

1. **Your Adventure Handbook:** This travel guide is like having a super helpful friend by your side. It's packed with all the info you need to explore Zanzibar's stunning beaches and conquer

Kilimanjaro's towering peak. We've researched so you can focus on having a blast!

2. **Expert Tips and Insights:** We've got insider tips that only the savviest travelers know. From the best times to visit what to pack and where to find the yummiest local food, we've got you covered.

3. **Guides and Pictures:** We know that sometimes words alone aren't enough. That's why we've included guides to help you find your way around, and eye-catching pictures so you can see exactly what to expect.

4. **Must-Read Chapters:** Each chapter is like a new adventure waiting for you. Whether you're into relaxing on the beach, exploring cool historical places, or reaching the top of Kilimanjaro, we've got chapters that will make you feel like a true explorer.

5. **Friendly and Easy Language:** We promise not to use confusing words or make things complicated. This guide is here to make your trip enjoyable and stress-free, so we're keeping it simple and fun to read.

6. **Create Your Journey:** Use this guide as a starting point to plan your exciting path. Mix and

match chapters to create the perfect adventure that fits your style.

So, get ready to embark on an incredible journey with this travel guide in your backpack. Whether you're a first-time traveler or a seasoned explorer, we're here to make sure you have an unforgettable experience in Zanzibar and Kilimanjaro. Let's get started!

Travel Tips and Safety Information

Embarking on a journey to Zanzibar and Kilimanjaro is an exciting adventure, but safety and preparedness are key. Here's a collection of valuable travel tips and safety information to ensure your trip is both enjoyable and secure:

1. **Health Precautions:**
   - Consult your healthcare provider before traveling to ensure you have the necessary vaccinations and medications.
   - Carry a basic first aid kit with essentials like bandages, pain relievers, and any necessary prescription medications.
   - Stay hydrated and consume safe, bottled water to avoid dehydration and stomach issues.

2. **Weather and Clothing:**
- Research the weather conditions in both Zanzibar and Kilimanjaro to pack appropriate clothing.
- Layer your clothing to adapt to changing temperatures, especially during the Kilimanjaro trek.
- Don't forget sunscreen, a wide-brimmed hat, and sunglasses to protect yourself from the sun's rays.

3. **Local Customs and Etiquette:**
- Learn a few basic phrases in Swahili to show respect for the local culture and connect with the people. (More in Chapter 8)
- Dress modestly when visiting religious sites or local communities to avoid offending local customs.

4. **Currency and Payments:**
- Familiarize yourself with the local currency and exchange rates before your trip. (More in Chapter 8)
- Carry a mix of cash and credit/debit cards for convenience and be cautious while using ATMs.

5. **Staying Connected:**
- Get a local SIM card or a portable Wi-Fi device to stay connected during your travels.

- Inform your family or friends about your travel plans and share your itinerary with them.

6. **Safety Measures:**
   - Be cautious with your belongings and use a money belt or secure bag to deter theft.
   - Avoid displaying valuable items like expensive jewelry or electronics in public places.
   - Use reputable transportation options and licensed tour operators to ensure your safety during excursions.
7. **Nature and Wildlife:**
   - Follow park regulations and guidelines when encountering wildlife in national parks.
   - Keep a safe distance from animals and avoid feeding them to prevent unexpected interactions.

8. **Altitude Sickness (For Kilimanjaro Trek):**
   - Acclimatize gradually during your trek to reduce the risk of altitude sickness.
   - Stay well-hydrated, eat nutritious meals, and communicate any discomfort to your guide.

9. **Emergency Contacts:**
   - Keep a list of important local contacts, including your country's embassy or consulate, emergency numbers, and the contact information of your accommodations.

10. **Travel Insurance:**
   - Purchase comprehensive travel insurance that covers medical emergencies, trip cancellations, and unexpected events.

Remember, your safety and well-being are top priorities. By following these travel tips and staying informed, you'll be better equipped to navigate your way through the wonders of Zanzibar and Kilimanjaro while enjoying a worry-free and enriching experience. Safe travels and happy exploring!

Chapter 2: Zanzibar: The Amazing Island in the Indian Ocean

Imagine a place that's like a treasure chest floating in the Indian Ocean. That's Zanzibar! With its sparkling blue waters and soft, sandy beaches, it's like a dream come true. But wait, there's more!

Zanzibar isn't just about beaches. It has a special town called Stone Town, where the buildings are like pages from a history book. Narrow streets, old houses, and colorful markets make you feel like you're stepping into the past.

And guess what? Zanzibar has a magic mix of cultures. People from all over the world came here, and their traditions blended like colors on an artist's palette. You'll taste new foods that will make your taste buds dance with joy!
So, if you're ready for a magical island adventure, Zanzibar is waiting with open arms. Get ready to dip your toes in the warm ocean, explore ancient streets, and create memories that will sparkle in your heart forever.

Exploring Zanzibar's Beautiful Beaches

Picture this: you're on a beach that looks like it came straight from a postcard. The sand is soft and warm beneath your feet, and the water is a stunning shade of blue. Welcome to Zanzibar's paradise beaches!

You can spend your days here doing whatever makes you happy. Build sandcastles, take a refreshing dip in the ocean, or simply relax under the shade of a swaying palm tree. The gentle breeze will kiss your skin, and the sound of the waves will be like a soothing lullaby.

Feeling adventurous? Snorkeling is like peeking into a whole new world underwater. Colorful fish dart around, and you might even spot a curious sea turtle gliding by. It's like being part of a nature documentary!

When it's time to refuel, you're in for a treat. Local food stalls offer mouthwatering dishes that will make your taste buds dance. Freshly caught seafood, tropical fruits, and spices make your senses tingle – every bite is an explosion of flavor.

As the sun sets, the sky turns into a canvas of oranges, pinks, and purples. It's a magical show that you won't want to miss. You can stroll along the shore, hand in hand with someone special, or simply sit and watch as the day fades into night.

Zanzibar's beaches aren't just beautiful; they're a piece of paradise that you can experience with all your senses. So pack your sun hat and sunglasses, and get ready for a beach adventure that will leave you with memories that sparkle like the ocean's waves.

Discovering Stone Town: A Journey into the Past with Illustrated Insights

Welcome to Stone Town, a place that's like a living time machine! Imagine walking through narrow streets lined with centuries-old buildings. It's like stepping back in time, and we're here to guide you through this fascinating adventure.
The Streets: Take a stroll through Stone Town's maze-like streets. The buildings are tall and close together like they're telling stories to each other. You'll notice intricate wooden doors with carvings that are like works of art.

Historic Houses: Let's step inside some of these amazing buildings. They're called "houses" but they're more like mini-palaces! Wooden balconies, big windows, and hidden courtyards – each house has its personality.
The Old Fort: Get ready to explore the Old Fort, a massive stone structure that's stood the test of time. It's like a fortress from a storybook, and you can even climb up for a view that's like a picture postcard.

Forodhani Gardens: After all that exploring, it's time for a break. Forodhani Gardens is like a green oasis in the heart of Stone Town. You can sit, relax, and enjoy the fresh air. And if you visit in the evening, you'll find a vibrant night market with tasty treats to try.

The House of Wonders: Get ready to be amazed by the House of Wonders. This grand building is like a palace of secrets. It's got a clock that's as big as a car, and inside, you'll discover Zanzibar's history and culture.

Local Life: Stone Town isn't just about buildings – it's also a place where people live and work. You'll see markets with colorful fruits and spices, and you can join the friendly locals as they go about their day.

So, get ready to step into Stone Town's time-traveling world. With every step, you'll uncover a new story and a piece of history. It's like being a detective on a fascinating quest, and we can't wait for you to unveil the secrets of this incredible place.

Practical Note: Remember to wear comfortable shoes for your exploration and keep a map handy to navigate the charming streets of Stone Town.

Immerse Yourself in Zanzibar's Vibrant Culture

Welcome to a world where colors are brighter, music is livelier, and every corner is a canvas of culture. Zanzibar's vibrant culture is waiting to embrace you in a warm and joyful embrace. Let's dive into this kaleidoscope of traditions, celebrations, and heartwarming moments.

Music and Dance: Get ready to move to the beat of Zanzibar's rhythm. Traditional music is like a language of its own, and you might find yourself swaying to taarab melodies or joining a lively dance performance. Imagine a night under the stars, surrounded by people laughing, clapping, and dancing to celebrate life.

Example: **Taarab Music:** Taarab is like a musical love story. The melodies are filled with emotions, and the lyrics tell tales of love, history, and everyday life. Imagine sitting in a courtyard, listening to the enchanting sounds of the qanun and oud as the singers share their stories.

Local Festivals: Zanzibar knows how to throw a party, and you're invited! From the Mwaka Kogwa New Year celebration to the Zanzibar International

Film Festival, there's always something exciting happening. It's a chance to mingle with locals, share laughter, and create unforgettable memories.

Example: **Mwaka Kogwa:** Imagine joining a playful water fight during Mwaka Kogwa. It's not just about splashing water; it's a way to release old grudges and start the year with a clean slate. You'll feel like a kid again as you chase your new friends with buckets of water!

Culinary Delights: Food is a big part of the culture, and Zanzibar's cuisine is a delicious journey in itself. Explore local markets bursting with exotic spices, tropical fruits, and fresh seafood. Don't miss out on a Swahili feast, where you'll savor dishes that have been passed down through generations.

Example: **Zanzibari Spices:** Take a guided spice tour to learn about the rich history of Zanzibar's spice trade. You'll see cinnamon, cloves, and vanilla growing in lush plantations. And who knows, you might even get to try some freshly prepared spice-infused dishes!

Art and Craftsmanship: Zanzibar is a hub of creativity, and you'll find talented artisans weaving magic with their hands. Explore local workshops to see intricate wood carvings, colorful textiles, and beautiful jewelry being crafted.

Example: **Woodcarving Workshops:** Visit a woodcarving workshop and watch skilled artists transform blocks of wood into stunning sculptures and intricate furniture. You might even get a chance to try your hand at carving your masterpiece.

Connecting with Locals: The heart of Zanzibar's culture is its people. Engage in friendly conversations, share stories, and experience the genuine warmth of the locals. Whether it's through a homestay, a visit to a village, or simply chatting with a market vendor, these interactions will leave a lasting impression.

Example: **Homestay Experience:** Imagine staying with a local family, learning how to prepare traditional dishes, and joining them for a meal. You'll gain a deeper understanding of daily life and forge connections that will stay with you long after you've left.

In Zanzibar, culture isn't just something you observe; it's something you become a part of. So, put on your dancing shoes, bring your appetite for adventure, and open your heart to the vibrant tapestry of Zanzibar's culture. It's a journey that will fill your soul with joy and leave you with stories to share for a lifetime.

Must-Try Local Cuisine and Culinary Delights

Imagine sitting at a wooden table, surrounded by the sounds of the ocean and the aroma of exotic spices filling the air. That was the scene when I dove into Zanzibar's incredible local cuisine, and let me tell you, it was like a flavor explosion I'll never forget.

Spice Markets and Aromas: My culinary adventure began at a bustling spice market. The air was thick with the scents of cardamom, cinnamon, and cloves. I couldn't resist picking up a handful of vibrant saffron threads and inhaling deeply, feeling like I was unlocking a treasure chest of flavors.

Seafood Delights: Zanzibar is a seafood lover's paradise, and oh boy, did I indulge! I savored a plate of grilled octopus that practically melted in my mouth. The spices used to season it added a delightful kick, making every bite a dance of flavors on my taste buds.

Street Food Magic: One evening, I ventured into a lively street food market. My eyes were drawn to a crowd gathered around a vendor flipping chapati, a local flatbread, on a hot griddle. I couldn't resist trying one – it was warm, flaky, and the perfect vehicle for scooping up rich and aromatic curries.

Zanzibari Breakfast: The mornings were a treat as well. I woke up to a traditional Zanzibari breakfast called "Vitumbua." These sweet and fluffy rice cakes were paired with a coconut and cardamom sauce that was like a warm hug for my taste buds.

Swahili Feast: The pinnacle of my culinary journey was a Swahili feast. Picture a table laden with dishes like pilau rice, tender marinated meats, and colorful vegetable stews. Each bite was a symphony of flavors – a bit of heat, a hint of sweetness, and a burst of aromatic spices.

Local Fruits: And how could I forget the tropical fruits? I devoured juicy slices of pineapple and mango that were so ripe and sweet, they tasted like pure sunshine.

Cooking Class Connection: To top it all off, I joined a cooking class to learn the art of Zanzibari cuisine. With a local chef as my guide, I pounded spices, chopped vegetables, and cooked up a storm. As I tasted the dishes I had prepared, I felt like

I had truly connected with the heart of Zanzibar's culture.

Zanzibar's cuisine isn't just about food – it's a journey through history, a celebration of flavors, and a connection to vibrant local life. So, when you visit this paradise, be sure to bring your appetite and an open heart. You're in for a culinary adventure that will awaken your senses and leave you with a newfound appreciation for the art of cooking.

Zanzibar Accommodation: Your Home Away from Home, Tailored to Your Style

When it comes to staying in Zanzibar, you're in for a delightful surprise – there's a place to rest your head that perfectly matches every kind of traveler. Whether you're a fan of luxury, a seeker of authenticity, or somewhere in between, Zanzibar's accommodation options have got you covered.

Luxury Resorts by the Sea: Imagine waking up to the gentle sound of waves and stepping onto your private terrace overlooking the turquoise ocean. Luxury resorts in Zanzibar are like dreams come true. With plush amenities, infinity pools, and beachfront access, you'll be pampered like royalty.

Cozy Boutique Hotels: If you're looking for a blend of comfort and character, boutique hotels in Zanzibar are the way to go. Picture yourself in a charming room with traditional Zanzibari decor, surrounded by lush gardens. It's like a hidden oasis where every corner tells a story.

Seaside Bungalows: Want to be right by the water's edge? Seaside bungalows offer a rustic charm that's hard to resist. You can practically roll out of bed and onto the sandy beach for a morning stroll or an afternoon dip in the ocean.

Eco-Friendly Retreats: For those who want to leave a smaller footprint, Zanzibar offers eco-friendly retreats that blend seamlessly with nature. Wake up to the sounds of birds and the rustling of leaves, knowing that your stay is contributing to the preservation of this beautiful island.

Historic Guesthouses: Get ready to step back in time with a stay in a historic guesthouse. These charming abodes are often tucked away in Stone Town's narrow streets, offering an authentic experience that's like living as a local. You'll find yourself surrounded by old-world charm and intriguing stories.

Homestays and Cultural Immersion: For a deeper dive into Zanzibar's culture, consider a homestay. Imagine becoming part of a Zanzibari family, sharing meals, stories, and laughter. It's a chance to forge meaningful connections and create memories that go beyond the typical tourist experience.

Practical Note: No matter where you choose to stay, it's a good idea to book in advance, especially during peak travel seasons. Keep in mind that

Zanzibar's accommodation options can vary in price, so there's something to suit every budget.

Whether you're seeking luxury, authenticity, or a little bit of both, Zanzibar's accommodation options are as diverse as its landscapes. So, pick the one that speaks to your heart, settle in, and get ready to make unforgettable memories on this enchanting island.

Chapter 3: Conquering Kilimanjaro

Kilimanjaro, Africa's tallest mountain, is a majestic challenge that beckons adventurers from around the world. This towering giant offers a journey through diverse landscapes and ecosystems, leading to the triumphant summit above the clouds.
As you ascend Kilimanjaro, you'll traverse through lush rainforests teeming with life, cross vast moorlands that stretch like a sea of golden grass, and push through otherworldly alpine deserts. Each step is a testament to your determination and resilience.

Choosing the right route is like selecting your path to glory. From the popular Machame Route to the quieter Lemosho Route, each trail offers its blend of stunning vistas and unique experiences.

The ultimate prize awaits at the summit, Uhuru Peak. At an astounding 5,895 meters (19,341 feet) above sea level, you'll stand on the roof of Africa, gazing at a panoramic view that stretches as far as the eye can see.

But conquering Kilimanjaro isn't just about the destination; it's about the journey itself. You'll form bonds with fellow trekkers, share stories with your guides, and immerse yourself in the mountain's captivating allure.
Practical Tips: Proper preparation, physical fitness, and acclimatization are key to a successful climb. Listening to your body, staying hydrated, and taking breaks is essential for a safe and enjoyable ascent.

Inspirational Note: Every step you take on Kilimanjaro is a step toward personal triumph. It's not just about reaching the summit; it's about embracing the challenge, discovering your inner strength, and realizing that you're capable of reaching new heights – both literally and metaphorically.

So, as you embark on this awe-inspiring journey, remember that Kilimanjaro isn't just a mountain – it's a testament to the human spirit, an emblem of courage, and a voyage that will leave you forever changed.

Mount Kilimanjaro: The Magnificent Monolith of Africa

Mount Kilimanjaro stands as a colossal sentinel on the Tanzanian horizon, casting its shadow over the land below. As Africa's highest peak, this dormant stratovolcano beckons adventurers and explorers to ascend its lofty heights.

Physical Marvel: Kilimanjaro's towering presence reaches an impressive 5,895 meters (19,341 feet) above sea level, making it the tallest freestanding mountain in the world. Its distinct snow-capped peak stands in stark contrast to the surrounding savannas and forests.

Ecological Diversity: The mountain's unique geographic location has fostered a range of ecosystems. The journey to the summit takes you through five distinct climatic zones, from the lush rainforests at the base to the arctic conditions near the peak. Along the way, you'll encounter diverse flora and fauna, each adapted to the specific conditions of its habitat.

Six Routes, One Destination: Kilimanjaro offers a variety of routes for trekkers to choose from, each providing a different perspective of the mountain's grandeur. Whether you opt for the well-traveled Machame Route or the scenic Rongai Route, the summit – known as Uhuru Peak – remains the ultimate goal.

Cultural Significance: Kilimanjaro holds cultural significance for the local Chagga people, who consider the mountain a sacred site. The mountain's name itself is believed to be derived from Swahili and Chagga words meaning "shining mountain."

A Journey of Discovery: Climbing Kilimanjaro is more than just a physical feat; it's an opportunity for self-discovery, perseverance, and personal triumph. Each step taken is a step towards reaching new heights, both literally and metaphorically.

Practical Note: Proper preparation, acclimatization, and a sense of adventure are essential for a successful climb. Hiring experienced guides and porters ensures a safe and enjoyable journey to the summit.

Inspirational Thought: As you stand at Uhuru Peak, gazing out across the vast African landscape, you'll feel a sense of accomplishment that goes beyond words. Mount Kilimanjaro is a testament to the power of human determination and the beauty of nature's grand design.

Choosing the Right Route: Your Path to Kilimanjaro's Summit

Embarking on a journey to Kilimanjaro's summit involves more than just lacing up your hiking boots. The route you choose will shape your experience, offering unique landscapes, challenges, and rewards. Let's navigate through the options to help you find the perfect path to your Kilimanjaro adventure.

1. **Machame Route:** Known as the "Whiskey Route," Machame is popular for its diverse scenery and gradual acclimatization. You'll traverse through lush rainforests, vast moorlands, and rocky terrain, all while enjoying stunning vistas along the way.

2. **Marangu Route:** Often called the "Coca-Cola Route," Marangu is the only route with hut accommodations. It offers a comfortable climb and well-defined paths, making it a good choice for those new to trekking.

3. **Lemosho Route:** This scenic route is known for its unspoiled wilderness and stunning panoramas. Longer and less crowded, Lemosho allows for better acclimatization and a more immersive experience.

4. **Rongai Route:** Starting from the north, Rongai offers a unique perspective of Kilimanjaro and is less crowded than other routes. It's a great choice for trekkers seeking a quieter journey.

5. **Northern Circuit Route:** The newest and longest route, Northern Circuit maximizes acclimatization with a gradual ascent. It offers unparalleled views and is ideal for those looking for an extended adventure.

6. **Umbwe Route:** For the daring and experienced, Umbwe is the steepest and most direct route. It's a challenging climb that requires excellent fitness and altitude tolerance.

Choosing Your Route: Practical Considerations

Fitness Level: Routes vary in difficulty, so assess your fitness and hiking experience before deciding.
- **Acclimatization:** Routes with longer durations allow for better acclimatization, increasing your chances of reaching the summit.
- **Crowd Preference:** Some routes see more trekkers than others. Decide if you prefer a quieter journey or enjoy the camaraderie of fellow adventurers.
- **Scenic Appeal:** Each route offers unique landscapes and views. Consider the scenery you'd like to experience along the way.
- **Time:** Routes vary in duration. Choose one that aligns with your schedule and allows for proper acclimatization.

Expert Tip: Regardless of the route, a positive attitude, proper gear, and adherence to your guide's advice are key to a successful climb.

Your choice of route is like selecting the chapters of your Kilimanjaro story. Whichever path you choose, remember that every step brings you closer to Kilimanjaro's summit – a triumph that will forever hold a place in your heart and memory.

Training and Preparation for Kilimanjaro Ascent

Climbing Kilimanjaro is a rewarding challenge, but it requires careful preparation and training to ensure a safe and successful ascent. Here's your guide to getting physically and mentally ready for this epic adventure:

Physical Fitness:

1. **Cardiovascular Endurance:** Build stamina through activities like hiking, jogging, cycling, and swimming. Aim for at least 30 minutes of aerobic exercise most days of the week.

2. **Strength Training:** Strengthen your core, legs, and upper body with weightlifting, squats, lunges, and push-ups. This will help you tackle the varied terrain of Kilimanjaro.

3. **Stair Climbing:** Kilimanjaro involves a lot of uphill trekking. Incorporate stair climbing into your routine to simulate the uphill sections of the climb.

4. **Long Walks:** Gradually increase the distance and duration of your walks to simulate the long trekking days on the mountain.

Mental Preparation:

1. **Positive Mindset:** Develop a positive attitude and mental resilience. Remind yourself of your goals and visualize yourself reaching the summit.

2. **Patience:** Kilimanjaro is a gradual ascent. Practice patience during your training and remember that slow and steady wins the race.
3. **Mental Endurance:** Train your mind to push through discomfort. This mental toughness will be invaluable during challenging moments on the mountain.

Altitude Acclimatization:

1. **Gradual Ascents:** Choose a route with a longer duration to allow for better acclimatization. Slowly increasing your elevation helps your body adjust to altitude.

2. **Practice Altitude:** If possible, spend time at higher altitudes before your climb to help your body adapt to reduced oxygen levels.

Gear and Equipment:

1. **Break-In Your Gear:** Wear your hiking boots and other gear on training hikes to ensure they're comfortable and won't cause blisters.

2. **Layering:** Experiment with different clothing layers to find the right combination for varying temperatures.

Hydration and Nutrition:

1. **Hydration:** Practice staying well-hydrated during your training hikes. Proper hydration is crucial for acclimatization and overall well-being.

2. **Nutrition:** Fuel your body with balanced meals, focusing on carbohydrates for sustained energy. Practice eating snacks during hikes to replicate on-trail eating.

Final Check:
1. **Medical Clearance:** Consult your doctor before embarking on a strenuous climb. Discuss any pre-existing conditions or concerns.
2. **Test Hikes:** Do a few longer hikes with your fully loaded backpack to simulate the conditions of Kilimanjaro.

Remember, the climb is not just about reaching the summit – it's about the journey itself. Embrace the challenges, stay committed to your training, and prepare both your body and mind for an unforgettable experience on Kilimanjaro. You've got this!

Experiencing the Flora and Fauna of Kilimanjaro's Ecosystems

Climbing Kilimanjaro isn't just a journey to the summit; it's a passage through a series of enchanting ecosystems, each teeming with unique flora and fauna. Get ready to be immersed in a world of natural wonders that will leave you awestruck.

Rainforest Realm:
As you start your ascent, you'll enter the rainforest zone. Tall trees form a lush canopy, creating a haven for countless species. Listen to the melodic chirping of birds and catch glimpses of playful monkeys swinging through the branches. Keep an eye out for Colobus monkeys, with their striking black and white fur.

Moorland Majesty:
Moving higher, you'll enter the moorland zone, where expansive grasslands stretch as far as the eye can see. Marvel at giant lobelias that resemble sculptures from another world. Look closely to spot the elusive and rare Kilimanjaro tree hyrax, a furry creature that calls these heights home.

Alpine Adventure:
As you ascend further, you'll reach the alpine desert. Here, life finds a way to thrive in harsh conditions. Look for resilient plants like the everlasting flower, which seems to defy the odds by blooming in the arid landscape. Keep your eyes peeled for the occasional mountain antelope, the klipspringer, gracefully navigating rocky outcrops.

Glacial Heights:
Approaching the summit, you'll encounter the chilling beauty of the glacial zone. While the glaciers themselves are diminishing, you'll still witness their grandeur. Keep an eye out for bird species adapted to high altitudes, such as the rufous-naped lark.

A Connection with Nature:
As you traverse through these diverse ecosystems, you'll develop a deeper appreciation for the delicate

balance of life on Kilimanjaro. Each step is a chance to connect with nature and witness the resilience of the plant and animal species that call this mountain home.

Practical Note: Remember to bring a pair of binoculars to enhance your wildlife spotting experience, and be respectful of the environment by following Leave No Trace principles.

Kilimanjaro isn't just a climb; it's a botanical and zoological adventure that will awaken your senses, enrich your understanding of the natural world, and leave you with a profound sense of wonder for the ecosystems that thrive in this extraordinary setting.

- Summiting Kilimanjaro: A Triumph of Will and Endurance

Standing at the threshold of Uhuru Peak, the culmination of your Kilimanjaro ascent, you'll come face to face with an indomitable sense of accomplishment. The journey to this summit is not just a climb; it's a testament to your willpower, endurance, and the human spirit's ability to conquer challenges.

The Midnight Trek:
The final push to the summit begins under a blanket of stars. With headlamps guiding the way, you'll embark on a nighttime ascent that requires mental fortitude. The biting cold and the thin air are no match for your determination.

Battle Against Altitude:
As you climb higher, the air becomes thinner, making each breath a triumph of adaptation. Your body's resilience shines through as you overcome altitude's challenges, step by step. You'll learn to pace yourself, listen to your body, and embrace the rhythm of your heartbeats.

Mental Resilience:
Summit night tests not only your physical strength but also your mental resilience. The darkness, the silence, and the knowledge that you're inching closer to the goal require unwavering focus. Doubts may creep in, but you'll silence them with your unwavering resolve.

Dawn's Glorious Arrival:
As the first light of dawn paints the sky with hues of gold and pink, you'll witness a breathtaking transformation. The world comes alive again, and you realize that you've conquered the night. Each

step toward the summit becomes a step closer to realizing your dream.

Triumph at the Top:
And then, the moment arrives. You stand at Uhuru Peak, gazing at the world below from the highest point in Africa. The feeling of triumph floods over you, a mixture of joy, relief, and an overwhelming sense of accomplishment. You've done it. You've conquered Kilimanjaro.

Summiting Kilimanjaro is more than just reaching the top; it's a profound journey of self-discovery, a testament to your inner strength, and a reminder that the human spirit knows no bounds. As you stand at Uhuru Peak, you'll realize that the mountain has not only tested your limits but has also unveiled the limitless potential that resides within you.

Chapter 4: Discovering Hidden Gems and Timeless Treasures

I knew I was in for a once-in-a-lifetime trip the minute I walked onto the beaches of Zanzibar. The island's colorful culture, gorgeous beaches, and ancient charm grabbed my heart, and I set out to uncover its must-see attractions and hidden jewels.

Walking Around Stone Town:
My first trip was to the enthralling Stone Town, where history is alive and well in every tight alley and elegant door. I marveled at the blend of Arabian, Indian, and African elements as I traveled through the labyrinthine alleyways. The aroma of spices remained in the air as I strolled through busy marketplaces, marveled at beautiful architecture, and immersed myself in the rich tapestry of cultures.

Tippu Tip House: Among the maze, I came to Tippu Tip House, a lesser-known jewel with a legendary background. This enormous palace, previously owned by a Swahili merchant, provided insight into Zanzibar's commercial history as well as the splendor of a bygone period.

Nungwi Beach Sunset Serenity:
As I continued north, I came to the powdery sands of Nungwi Beach. The blue waves spread out before me in front of me, and I couldn't resist the lure of the sea. I spent my days soaking up the rays, snorkeling amid the vibrant coral reefs, and closing each day with a breathtaking sunset that painted the sky in orange and pink colors.

Kendwa Rocks: A little distance away, I discovered Kendwa Rocks, a refuge of peace and leisure. I delighted in the calming rhythms of the water, swinging on a hammock as my anxieties faded.

Taking the Spice Road:
A trip to Zanzibar would be incomplete without a visit to the spice farms. Touching, smelling, and tasting unique spices that have molded Zanzibar's character for millennia, I began on a sensory journey. The Spice Tour not only pleased my senses but also expanded my knowledge of the island's rich history.

Mchangamble Village: Among the verdant plantations, I came upon Mchangamble Village, a place where time appeared to stand still. I enjoyed laughs, tales, and a typical Swahili supper with the kind natives, which warmed my spirit.

Jambiani Cultural Immersion:
My voyage brought me to Jambiani, a fishing town on Zanzibar's shore, where I encountered the essence of coastal life. I participated in traditional fishing displays, studied the skill of seaweed cultivation, and danced to the rhythmic rhythms of taarab music.

Dolphin Watching at Kizimkazi: at Kizimkazi, I had the honor of swimming with gorgeous dolphins in their natural environment, an experience that left me awestruck and deeply affected.

Reflecting on My Experience:
As my time in Zanzibar drew to an end, I found myself pondering on the beauty I had seen and the friendships I had made. Zanzibar had left an indelible mark on my heart, from the busy streets of Stone Town to the tranquil beaches and lovely villages. It was a trip of discovery, a cultural festival, and an investigation of hidden riches that would be woven into the fabric of my recollections for the rest of my life.

Serengeti National Park: Witness Nature's Greatest Show

The primitive dance of hundreds upon thousands of creatures dictates the pace of existence in the heart of Tanzania. This is Serengeti National Park, and the scene has been prepared for the incredible sight known as the Great Migration.

The Life Cycle Unfolds:

Imagine boundless savannas reaching as far as the eye can see, with the shifting seasons orchestrating the ebb and flow of life. The Great Migration is a cyclical trek in which millions of wildebeests, zebras, and gazelles travel the Serengeti in search of new grazing grounds and water supplies.

The River Bridges:
The river crossings are one of the most spectacular and heart-pounding parts of the trek. The suspense is palpable as the herds try to negotiate the perilous crocodile-infested waterways. A single jump may be the difference between safety and peril, and seeing this survival of the fittest is both fascinating and humbling.

On the Prowl for Predators:
The Great Migration is more than simply a show for herbivores. The Serengeti's predators - lions, cheetahs, and leopards - are feasting. These apex predators are waiting in the wings, ready to take advantage of the bounty provided by the migration. The conflict between predator and prey adds another level of drama to this natural theater.

A Life and Renewal Circle:
The Great Migration exemplifies the circle of life, serving as a striking reminder of nature's cycles of birth, survival, and regeneration. It's a living witness to the delicate balance that keeps ecosystems alive, as well as a powerful picture of the wild's beauty and ferocity.

Seeing the Wonder:
Seeing the Great Migration means seeing one of the world's greatest natural marvels. Whether you witness it from a safari vehicle or the sky in a hot air balloon, the encounter is a sobering reminder of the natural world's majesty and intricacy.
Practical Note: Because the date of the migration changes from year to year, arranging your visit around the prime migration months (July to October) maximizes your chances of viewing this incredible phenomenon.

You are not simply a spectator at Serengeti National Park; you are a participant in the everlasting rhythm of the wild. The Great Migration is a living symphony, a chapter in nature's tale that will leave you in awe of the planet we call home.

Ngorongoro Crater: Nature's Conservation and Diversity Masterpiece

Consider a world in which animals roam free in a submerged paradise surrounded by the towering walls of an old volcanic crater. This is Ngorongoro Crater, a natural marvel whose pristine beauty and biodiversity have been maintained thanks to extraordinary conservation efforts.

A Geological Wonder:
A major volcanic explosion built a wide crater over two million years ago, forming Ngorongoro Crater. Today, this geological wonder is home to a unique and self-contained environment that sustains an incredible variety of fauna.

A Wildlife Refuge:
When you descend into the crater, you'll find yourself surrounded by a genuine Noah's Ark of creatures. Lions, elephants, rhinos, buffalo, and a variety of other animals thrive in the different ecosystems, which range from broad grasslands to deep forests. It's a microcosm of Africa's famous species, all coexisting peacefully.

Conservation Victory:
Ngorongoro Crater is a shining example of excellent conservation initiatives. Its classification as a UNESCO World Heritage Site and protected area assures that this natural gem stays unspoiled by human intrusion, enabling future generations to marvel at its beauty.

Cultural Interactions:
Ngorongoro Crater is a cultural crossroads in addition to its spectacular vistas and animals. The Maasai people, who have coexisted with animals for years, graze their livestock around the crater's rim, a living monument to human-nature harmony.

Once in a Lifetime Safari:
Exploring the Ngorongoro Crater is like going on a safari through a wildlife paradise. Every bend along its rails exposes a fresh story in the lives of its residents. Every moment is a brushstroke in nature's masterpiece, from the gentle giants grazing quietly to the sneaky predators on the hunt.

Practical Note: Visiting Ngorongoro Crater needs a permit and is best done with the assistance of a competent guide who can negotiate the terrain and give insights into the crater's ecosystem.

Ngorongoro Crater is more than just a tourist attraction; it's a living monument to nature's design and the power of conservation. It evokes the beauty that develops when humans and the wilderness strike a peaceful balance, transforming it into a place of wonder, inspiration, and thankfulness for the natural world's splendors.

Tarangire National Park: Home to Elephants

A world develops in the heart of Tanzania, where the animal kingdom's giants wander free, providing a beautiful image of wild beauty. Tarangire National

Park is a haven where elephants take center stage and nature emanates its unadulterated beauty.
The Giant Land:
When you arrive at Tarangire, you will be met with scenery unlike any other. The bizarre shadows of ancient baobab trees against the horizon are created by their strive for the sky. The magnificent elephants, though, steal the show, dotting the savanna-like living monuments to elegance and might.
Gatherings of Elephants:
Tarangire is famous for having one of the world's greatest populations of elephants. When water is limited during the dry season, these gentle giants congregate along the Tarangire River in a stunning demonstration of community and survival.

The Life Dance:
You'll see charming behaviors as you monitor the elephants' sophisticated social connections, from sensitive moments between mother and calf to loud play among the young. Each action demonstrates their intellect and range of emotions.

A Wildlife Symphony:
Tarangire's roster of characters includes more than just elephants. Lions stalk through the grass, giraffes reach gracefully for leaves, while wildebeests and zebras roam the plains. The air is filled with bird sounds, completing the symphony of the wild.

The Excitement of Safari:
Exploring Tarangire is an immersive experience, with game drives providing close encounters with these amazing species. With each turn, you'll discover moments that will captivate you, capturing the spirit of Africa's wild soul.

Practical Tip: The dry season (June to October) is the greatest time to see Tarangire's elephant herds and rich wildlife.
Tarangire National Park is more than simply a site; it's a monument to nature's majesty and a celebration of the magnificent wildlife that call it

home. Amidst the baobabs and golden grasslands, elephants wander like monarchs, reminding us of the awe-inspiring beauty that lies beyond our daily lives.

Lake Manyara and its Abundant Bird Diversity

Lake Manyara, nestled inside Tanzania's lap, is a calm paradise that calls with its placid waters and beautiful surroundings. The lake's vast avian variety converts it into a sanctuary for bird aficionados, but it's the sky above and the waters below that steal the show.

Peacock Symphony:
The beaches of Lake Manyara come alive with a stunning assortment of bird species, each contributing its note to a symphony of colors and songs. Every winged resident adds to a tapestry of bird magnificence, from the vivid flash of kingfishers to the smooth glide of pelicans.

Flamingo Madness:
Lake Manyara is famous for its gorgeous pink inhabitants, who include hundreds of flamingos that wade in its shallows. Their coordinated

motions produce a stunning dance, coloring the seas in almost surreal pink hues.

Raptors in the Air:
Raptors command the air over the lake. These predators attract attention as they fly, hunt, and demonstrate their aerial skills, from magnificent eagles to sneaky hawks.

A Photographer's Dream:
Lake Manyara provides photographers with a plethora of shot options. In this avian paradise, capturing the delicate features of a bird in flight or the tranquil quiet of one seated by the water's side has become an art form.

Practical Tip: For the finest birding chances, visit Lake Manyara National Park during the dry season (June to October).

Lake Manyara is more than simply a body of water; it's a haven of feathers and song, a domain where the bird world takes center stage. You'll be greeted by a dazzling exhibition of nature's creative palette as you walk along its banks, a reminder of the endless variety that adorns our planet's landscapes.

Adventures Off the Beaten Path: Uncovering Tanzania's Best-Kept Secrets

Tanzania contains a treasure trove of hidden jewels waiting to be explored beyond the well-trodden routes and known sights. Explore the lesser-known marvels that make this nation exceptional on an off-the-beaten-path excursion.

The Kingdom of Kipunji:
The Kipunji monkey, an elusive primate, roams the deep woods of the Southern Highlands. This beautiful species, found only in Tanzania, captivates with its distinct sounds and lively antics. A visit to their natural home provides a look into a world unspoiled by time.

The Unknown Kitulo Plateau:
The Kitulo Plateau, often known as the "Serengeti of Flowers," blooms with a kaleidoscope of wildflowers, rivaling any
floral paradise. This hidden treasure is a botany enthusiast's dream, providing a tranquil getaway into nature's palette.

Enchanted Trails of Udzungwa:
Explore the Udzungwa Mountains to see lush rainforests and gushing waterfalls. Hiking through the lush terrain of Udzungwa shows a wealth of variety, including uncommon monkeys, colorful birds, and peculiar plant species.

Pangani's Coastal Attractions:
Get away from the throng and visit Pangani, a beach village where time appears to stand still. Explore its old architecture, walk along unspoiled beaches, and take a boat ride to Maziwe Island Marine Reserve for snorkeling in crystal-clear seas.

Ruaha's Rugged Beauty:
Ruaha National Park provides a harsh and pristine terrain for people looking for untamed wildness. Ruaha, with its abundant species and spectacular terrain, offers a true safari experience away from the masses.

Practical Note: To guarantee a safe and fulfilling experience, exploring these hidden gems frequently requires careful preparation and local understanding.

Tanzania's hidden gems reflect the country's diverse landscapes, animals, and civilizations.

Exploring these off-the-beaten-path activities rewards the adventurous visitor with a better grasp of Tanzania's essence and a collection of memories that will last a lifetime.

Chapter 5: Exploring the Best of the Zanzibar Coast

The coastline of Zanzibar, with its gorgeous beaches, turquoise oceans, and unique cultural history, invites visitors to embark on an extraordinary voyage along its coasts. Exploring the finest of the Zanzibar Coast reveals a tapestry of experiences that weave natural beauty, historical history, and engaging cultural interactions together.

Tropical Paradise Is Calling:
The coastline of Zanzibar is a sanctuary for beachgoers and sunbathers. Endless lengths of powdered sand meet the turquoise Indian Ocean to create picture-perfect landscapes that promote relaxation and refreshment. From the vibrant coastlines of Nungwi to the serenity of Paje, each beach has its distinct personality, providing a chance to relax among breathtaking scenery.

Cultural Intersections:
The history of the Zanzibar Coast has been influenced by centuries of marine commerce and cultural contact. The UNESCO World Legacy Site Stone Town is a living testimony to this legacy. Its winding alleyways, elaborate doorways, and antique structures reflect the story of Swahili, Arabic, and

European influences that have weaved the fabric of Zanzibar's character.

Dhows and More:
Exploring the seaside is more than simply lying on beaches; it's also a chance to immerse oneself in true marine customs. Setting sail aboard a traditional dhow provides an insight into Zanzibar's previous nautical life. From fishing expeditions to sunset cruises, these wooden boats provide a unique viewpoint on the beauty of the coastline.

Culinary Journey:
The coastal cuisine of Zanzibar is a combination of tastes inspired by the island's unique cultural past. As you indulge in traditional cuisine, savor fragrant spices, fresh fish, and exotic fruits. The Zanzibar Coast encourages you to tempt your taste senses and go on a gastronomic journey that reflects the region's unique cultural tapestry.

Vibrant Marine Life:
The Zanzibar Coast serves as a doorway to an underwater paradise. Snorkeling and diving in its clear waters show spectacular coral gardens rich with marine life. Swim alongside colorful fish, beautiful sea turtles, and even dolphins to connect with the wonders of the Indian Ocean.

Sunsets and balmy breezes:
The Zanzibar Coast changes into a land of ethereal beauty when the sun sets below the horizon. Palm palms rustle in the air, while the sky is painted in orange and pink colors. Sunset strolls along the beach transform into lyrical moments of peace, the ideal cap to each day's coastal exploration.

Tip: When visiting the Zanzibar Coast, respect local traditions, promote sustainable tourism practices, and follow marine conservation rules.

Exploring the greatest of the Zanzibar Coast is an expedition of natural beauty, cultural wealth, and endless leisure. The Zanzibar Coast provides a canvas where your fantasies meet the dazzling seas of the Indian Ocean, whether you're looking for adventure, history, or just a calm retreat.

Zanzibar's Magnificent Beaches: Where White Sands Meet Crystal Waters

Imagine walking onto a beach with sand the color of snow and water so pure you can see to the bottom. Welcome to the magnificent beaches of Zanzibar, a sanctuary where nature portrays a picture of perfect beauty.

The Sands of Time:
The beaches of Zanzibar are like something out of a fairy tale. It's like walking on a cloud since the sand is so silky and thin. You may sink your toes into the fine sands and create tracks that the gentle waves rapidly obliterate. It's the kind of joy that can only be found on a genuinely wonderful beach.

Crystalline Water:
Then there's the water - the water! It's similar to peering into a crystal ball. The water is so pure that you can see the fish swimming under the surface as if asking you to join them in their underwater world. Blue and green colors dance together in a captivating tango that is difficult to ignore.

Beachfront Paradise:
Consider yourself relaxing on a comfy beach chair, with the sun caressing your skin and a soft wind rustling through your hair. The beach spreads out in front of you, a painting of tranquility and leisure. Listen to the relaxing sounds of the sea, read a book, or just let your mind wander.

An Activity Playground:
Zanzibar's beaches aren't simply for relaxing; they're also a playground for adventurers. You may go snorkeling and experience a world of vibrant

corals and aquatic life. Maybe you want to experience the exhilaration of skimming over the sea on a kiteboard. Zanzibar's beaches provide something for everyone, whether you're an adventurer or a thrill-seeker.

Magic of the Sunset:

As the day draws to a close, the beach turns into a stage for one of nature's most spectacular shows: the sunset. The sky transforms into a kaleidoscope of warm oranges, pinks, and purples, giving a lovely light over the sea. It's a magical moment you'll remember for the rest of your life.

The gorgeous beaches of Zanzibar are more than simply places to visit; they are places to experience, feel a profound connection with nature's beauties, and make memories that will last a lifetime. It's a spot where white dunes and clear seas combine to produce a symphony of beauty that is just beyond description.

Zanzibar Water Adventure: A Symphony of Snorkeling, Diving, and Water Sports

I felt the ocean's pull as I stepped onto Zanzibar's beaches, a siren song of adventure that took me to a world of undersea delights. Every minute of my Zanzibar water adventure was exciting, from snorkeling through coral gardens to diving into the depths and even trying my hand at exhilarating water sports.

Snorkeling Treasures:
I walked into the crystal-clear waters, mask and snorkel in hand, anxious to explore the undersea kingdom. A whole new universe opened up underneath me as I floated on the surface. Schools of brightly colored fish swam over beautiful coral formations, each one seeming to be more

enthralling than the previous. It felt like being a part of a magical aquatic ballet.

Diving to the Deep:
Taking my voyage a step further, I participated in a scuba diving expedition that took me far into the Indian Ocean. The soft currents were the only thing breaking the stillness as I fell. I felt like an adventurer uncovering a secret kingdom as I swam among the corals. I marveled at the rich elements that made up this underwater tapestry as the vivid marine life appeared to welcome me into their home.

Amazing Water Sports:
I entered the world of water sports to get an adrenaline high. Kiteboarding enabled me to harness the strength of the wind, skimming over the water's surface with a sense of ecstasy. As I slashed through the waves, the wind pushed at my kite, giving me a sensation of freedom I'd never felt before.

Beach Bliss and Sunset Magic:
I took refuge on Zanzibar's peaceful beaches after days of water exploration. I looked in astonishment as the sun set below the horizon and the sky turned into a tapestry of brilliant colors. The smooth waves

of the ocean created a peaceful soundtrack, and I realized that the enchantment of Zanzibar's waters continued to weave its spell even on the beach.

My Zanzibar water journey was a symphony of feelings, a kaleidoscope of hues, and a profound connection with the ocean's secrets. Each moment engraved a new chapter in my trip, reminding me of the vast beauty that exists under the waters and beyond the coast, from the brilliant reefs to the adrenaline of water sports and the peace of the beach.

Dive into Zanzibar's Marine Masterpiece: Vibrant Reefs and Enchanting Creatures

A world of incomparable beauty lies under the surface of Zanzibar's pristine seas - a region where colorful corals flourish and a varied cast of marine animals dance in a symphony of life. Exploring Zanzibar's marine life and coral reefs invites you to enter an underwater realm that is beyond description.

The Unveiling of the Coral Kingdoms:
As I sank into the depths, I was greeted with the coral reefs' kaleidoscope of hues. It seemed like an

artist's palette had been strewn over the ocean bottom. Towering coral structures extended toward the sun, their unique forms and textures sheltering a fascinating assortment of aquatic life. Each species, from tiny fan corals to enormous brain corals, had made its spot in this underwater paradise.

A Vibrant Creature Tapestry:
Life pulsated with bright intensity among the corals. Schools of fish rushed into and out of crevices, their scales gleaming like gems in the embrace of the sea. Sea turtles floated gracefully through the currents, their ancient presence a reminder of the ocean's ageless secrets. Then there were the smaller species, such as tiny nudibranchs, elusive seahorses, and camouflaged octopuses, all testaments to nature's limitless inventiveness.

Hunting and Being Hunted:
The delicate balance of predator and prey played out in a quiet dance in this aquatic wonderland. While elegant sharks patrolled the deeper worlds, camouflaged lionfish tracked their prey with graceful accuracy. Even in the thick of the hunt, there was a feeling of harmony - a reminder that every species had a part to perform in this complex web of existence.

Coral Conservation and Stewardship:
While the reefs of Zanzibar are beautiful, they are also vulnerable ecosystems that need our care. Responsible research and environmentally friendly activities are critical to conserving the reefs for future generations. I was reminded of the necessity of conserving this undersea sanctuary from the risks of pollution, overfishing, and climate change as I gazed at the marine life.

Exploring the marine life and coral reefs of Zanzibar is a luxury that reveals the mystery of the ocean's depths. Each dive is a trip into a realm of limitless beauty, where every twist and turn unveils a new masterpiece. It's a journey of discovery that develops a profound respect for the wonders of the undersea environment as well as a dedication to preserving its riches for future generations.

My Heartfelt Journey: Embracing Zanzibar's Local Fishing Communities

I went on a very rewarding adventure within the vivid tapestry of Zanzibar's culture - meeting with the local fishing community who have woven their lives into the island's coastal rhythms. I encountered a world of genuineness, perseverance, and emotional relationships when I delved beyond the tourist traps, and it left an unforgettable impression on my spirit.

By the Dhows in the Mornings:
One early morning, I found myself on the beaches of a little fishing community, where traditional dhows stood sentinels on the beach. The local fisherman smiled and invited me to join them on their boats as they prepared for a day of fishing. We set sail as the sun rose, the beat of the waves reflecting the cadence of their chants.

Storytelling and Casting Nets:
I observed a skillful dance on the show as the fisherman threw their nets with accuracy developed over centuries. I felt a feeling of togetherness with their effort as the nets unfolded and splashed into the ocean - a common connection to the sea that nourishes their life. In between casts, they told me about their families, their catches, and the difficulties they encounter.

Traditions and Mending Nets:
Back on shore, I had the honor of helping the fisherman fix their nets. I sat cross-legged on the sand, listening closely as they told stories of their ancestors and the rituals handed down through centuries. Their laughing and camaraderie

exemplified the close-knit relationships that characterize their community.

Bounty Sharing:
After the day's labor, I was welcomed to a communal supper with the fishing families. Our dishes were adorned with freshly caught fish that had been cooked to perfection. The tastes explode with sea essence, a gourmet celebration of their everyday labor. It was a sobering event, a reminder that nourishment and friendship are intertwined in their lives.

A Touching Connection:
My stay in Zanzibar's fishing settlements was more than just a cultural exchange; it was a meaningful connection to the island's heart. I acquired insight into the obstacles they encounter and the perseverance that characterizes their spirit via their tales, traditions, and everyday routines. This event changed my journey into one of empathy and understanding, reminding me of the common threads that connect us all as people.

Engaging with Zanzibar's indigenous fishing villages was a window into the essence of a place, a treasured memory of shared laughter, and an everlasting reminder of the power of genuine human relationships.

Sunsets and Stargazing: Unforgettable Coast Moments

Every dusk on the shore of Zanzibar, a wonderful metamorphosis occurs. As the sun starts to set, painting the sky with warm orange and gold colors, I find myself attracted to the seashore, ready to see an exquisite show.

Sundowner Serenade:
Standing on the beach, I feel a pleasant wind on my skin as I watch the sun drop lower and lower, creating an almost surreal tapestry of hues. The waves seem to be dancing to hidden music, in time with the sun's sinking. Each passing instant is like a stroke of a painter's brush, and I am mesmerized by nature's craftsmanship.

A Starry Blanket:
As the sun sets, a new heavenly drama starts to play out. The sky darkens, exposing a tapestry of stars glittering like diamonds against a velvety background. I am treated to an astronomy spectacle far away from the city lights that is just magnificent.

The Milky Way spans the sky, and constellations come to life like I've never seen before.

Coastal Romance:
I lay on the beach and let the waves sing to me with their gentle beat. I feel a feeling of serenity sweeps over me with each wave that brushes the coast. I'm buried in ideas as wide as the cosmos itself, while the stars overhead glimmer like faraway lanterns. It's a time for reflection and amazement, an opportunity to connect with the universe.

Eternal Connection:
During such beautiful times, I am reminded of how insignificant I am in this enormous world and how intertwined everything is. The sun that set over Zanzibar continues to shine in other regions. The same stars that illuminate the night sky have seen many historical events. And here, on the beaches of Zanzibar, I am a part of that ageless story.

Sunsets and stargazing on the shore of Zanzibar have left me with wonderful memories. They've taught me to appreciate the beauty of the present moment, to marvel at the natural world's grandeur, and to find peace in the simple but deep delights that life has to offer. As the sun sets below the horizon and the stars glitter overhead, I am reminded that some of life's most treasured moments are discovered when the world slows down and we are left to wonder at the universe's magnificence.

Chapter 6: Immersion in Tanzanian Culture

When you enter Tanzania, you are entering a world of vivid customs, engaging tales, and warm-hearted people. Immersion in Tanzanian culture is a journey that weaves together the strands of history, art, music, and daily life.

Friendly greetings and smiles:
You will be welcomed with genuine smiles from the time you arrive. Tanzanians are recognized for their hospitality, and you will feel as if you are a member of their extended family. You'll feel the warmth and openness that characterize Tanzanian culture whether you're having a cup of chai (tea) or participating in a vibrant dance.

Traditional Flavors:
Prepare your taste buds! Tanzanian cuisine is a taste combination that tells the narrative of the country and its people. Every meal provides a delectable look into the country's culinary past, from the savory deliciousness of nyama choma (grilled beef) to the fragrant spices of pilau (spiced rice). Don't miss out on popular street cuisine, such as mishikaki (meat skewers) and mandazi (fried flatbread).

Vibrant Markets and Handicrafts:
Exploring local markets is a sensory experience. The booths are filled with colorful textiles, handmade jewelry, and elaborate sculptures, showing the craftsmanship of Tanzanian artists. You'll be able to take home a piece of the culture, whether it's a lovely kanga (wrap) or a Makonde carving that tells a story.

Life Rhythms:
Tanzanian music and dancing are like the nation's pulse. Drums, hip swaying, and beautiful songs create an appealing beat that begs you to participate in the celebration. You'll be carried up in the joyful spirit of Tanzanian music whether you're learning the techniques of the ngoma dance or listening to the sounds of traditional instruments.

Honoring Traditions:
Tanzanian culture is strongly founded on traditions and beliefs handed down from generation to generation. Each village has its distinct personality, from the Maasai warriors' vivid dress to the seaside Swahili traditions. When you participate in these customs, you are not only watching; you are also demonstrating respect for the values that create Tanzanian life.

A Language Tapestry:
In Tanzania, Swahili is the language of communication. A few words or phrases learned may lead to meaningful discussions and genuine friendships. The simple act of greeting someone with "Jambo!" (Hello!) may result in smiles and cross-cultural dialogues.
Immersion in Tanzanian culture is a voyage of discovery in which every meeting, taste, and conversation becomes a brushstroke in a vibrant painting. It's an invitation to go under the surface and connect with the country's spirit, to hear its tales, and to become a part of its live tapestry of traditions and experiences.

Traditional Tanzanian Music, Dance, and Festivals

Music and dance are more than simply forms of entertainment in Tanzania; they are dynamic manifestations of the country's rich cultural history. Traditional Tanzanian music and dance weave a tapestry of celebration that draws people together and relates tales from the past, with rhythmic rhythms and vibrant motions.

Resonant Rhythms:
Tanzanian music is a symphony of sounds that represent the country's rich fabric of communities. Traditional instruments like drums, xylophones, and flutes combine to produce vibrant tunes. The rhythms are contagious, and even if you've never danced before, you'll find yourself swaying to the beat.

Expression Dances:
Dance is an important component of Tanzanian culture, serving as a means of expressing pleasure, ceremonies, and storytelling. Each location has its distinct dancing style, with motions that reflect the natural environment, ranging from the delicate swaying of palm trees to the energetic jumps of animals. Dancing is a language that transcends words, whether it's the Maasai leaping dance or the fast-paced kiganda.

Festivals that Bring People Together:
Tanzania comes alive with lively festivals that celebrate its culture and customs throughout the year. The Zanzibar International Film Festival (ZIFF) celebrates African film and creative skill, while the Bagamoyo Arts Festival brings together a diverse group of artists, musicians, and performers. Makonde, one of the most well-known festivals,

brings communities together to remember their ancestors via song, dancing, and ceremony.

Voice Harmony:
Tanzanians put a high value on vocal music. Melodic melodies and strong voices combine to produce songs that depict tales of love, history, and everyday life. Choirs and groups often sing in Swahili, the national language, which adds a sense of togetherness to the music.

Traditions to Pass Down:
Tanzanian music, dance, and festivals are more than simply forms of entertainment; they are containers of tradition handed down from generation to generation. Children learn their ancestors' songs and dances, ensuring that the rhythms of the past continue to echo in the present. This link to one's ancestors lends depth and significance to every note and stride.

Tanzanian music, dance, and festivals are a dynamic witness to the country's cultural richness as well as the spirit of solidarity that draws people together to celebrate. By watching these exuberant manifestations, you are not just witnessing a performance, but also being a part of a centuries-old tradition that celebrates life, tales, and Tanzania's pulse.

Exploring Zanzibar's Local Arts and Crafts

Zanzibar is an artistic treasure trove, where the hands of talented artists produce a kaleidoscope of colors, textures, and tales. Visiting its markets and workshops is an invitation to experience the wonder of creation and take a bit of the island's spirit home with you.

Bright Markets:
The crowded marketplaces of Zanzibar are a sensory overload. The stalls are brimming with vivid textiles, complex sculptures, and gleaming jewels. The Darajani Market in Stone Town is a sensory experience, with spices creating a fragrant tapestry and traders beckoning you to examine their wares. Everything from beautiful hand-woven baskets to fascinating artworks that reflect the soul of the island may be found here.

Craft Workshops:
When you go deeper, you'll find the core of Zanzibar's creative tradition in its workshops. Skilled artisans convert raw materials into works of

art, showing their abilities in woodcarving, weaving, and beading. Visiting a workshop is like gazing into the head of an artist, where creativity and tradition collide.

Curiosities from Zanzibar:
The Mwenge Craft Market, located in the center of Stone Town, is a refuge for oddities reflecting Zanzibar's culture. Hand-carved masks depict ancestral spirits, while vibrant kanga textiles feature elaborate patterns with secret significance. Exploring these marketplaces is an experience in and of itself, as you find treasures from Zanzibar's past.

The Batik Story:
The art of batik is one of Zanzibar's distinctive creative heritage. This old process may be seen in action at the Zanzibar Curio Shop. Artists make elaborate designs on cloth using wax and dye, resulting in vivid textiles that are not only attractive but also communicate tales about the island's history and traditions.

Traditions of Carving:
The Zanzibar Butterfly Centre immerses you in the realm of woodcarving. Artists carve slabs of wood into elaborate patterns that depict the island's

vegetation and animals. The precise accuracy of their work is breathtaking, and you'll get to see the creation of sculptures that symbolize Zanzibar's natural beauty.

Exploring Zanzibar's unique arts and crafts is a voyage of discovery, providing an opportunity to see the talent, passion, and imagination that characterize the island's cultural environment. With each step through marketplaces and workshops, you'll be immersed in a world where art serves as a bridge between the past and the present, and where the vivid spirit of Zanzibar comes to life in every handcrafted creation.

Embracing Zanzibar's Heartfelt Hospitality: Meeting Warm and Friendly Locals

My trip to Zanzibar was more than simply a hunt for magnificent scenery and
breathtaking beaches; it was also a chance to engage with the people who live in this island paradise. I was greeted by the warmth and genuine kindness of the residents from the time I set foot on its beaches, generating moments of connection that will live on in my heart.

A Simple Welcome:
I was impressed by the simplicity of a welcome as I went through Stone Town's small lanes. A cheery "Jambo!" (Hello!) from a passing local sparked a chat that cut beyond linguistic boundaries. We laughed, told tales, and exchanged a few Swahili words, forming an immediate link that reminded me of the strength of a genuine connection.

Invited into Residences:
While touring a seaside town one evening, I was lured to the sounds of laughing and music emanating from a small cottage. Curiosity brought me to its front door, where I was greeted by a family making a traditional supper. They gladly welcomed me to join them, and I got to experience the thrill of exchanging tales over a communal meal firsthand.

Crafting Relationships:
I realized at the crowded marketplaces that a genuine interest in local goods and customs opens the door to meaningful encounters. The artists excitedly revealed the history behind their products as I admired the beautiful carvings and vivid materials. Learning about the meaning of each design increased my admiration and generated cross-cultural interactions.

Dancing with Friends:
I was intrigued by the rhythms of traditional music and dancing on a seaside evening. I joined the celebrations with a little prodding, dancing alongside locals who greeted me with open arms. We spoke a common language of delight via laughing and dancing, and I felt a feeling of togetherness that was beyond words.

A Goodbye with Memories:

As my stay in Zanzibar drew to a conclusion, I recognized that the relationships I had made with the natives were the genuine jewels of my trip. Bidding goodbye was difficult, but I knew that the memories of shared laughter, deep talks, and cultural exchanges would last a lifetime.

My time in Zanzibar taught me that getting to know the friendly natives is more than simply visiting a place - it's about immersing oneself in a world of true human relationships. We may build bridges of understanding and friendships that transcend countries and cultures by accepting their hospitality, opening our hearts, and participating in meaningful exchanges.

Taking part in cultural exchanges and homestays

During my journey to Zanzibar, I decided to engage in cultural exchanges and homestays, which turned out to be one of the most enlightening and changing experiences of my life. It wasn't only about seeing the sites; it was about being a part of the community, participating in their daily lives, and learning about their culture.

Greetings as Family:
When I arrived in the local hamlet, I was received cordially by my host family, who treated me as if I were one of their own. The genuine smiles and open arms immediately made me feel at ease, and I knew this was the start of an unforgettable experience.

A Taste of the Past:
Mealtimes were a treasured occasion to experience not only the delectable tastes of Tanzanian food but also the tales and customs that accompanied each dish. My host family gently taught me how to cook traditional dishes, explaining their culinary secrets as well as the importance of the ingredients. We sat around a communal table, breaking bread and laughing together, forming a bond that transcends cultural barriers.

Learning via Experience:
I enjoyed the routine of rural life, from early duties to nighttime rituals. I assisted with animal care, agricultural chores, and talks that provided me with a better understanding of their way of life. I learned from these shared experiences that genuine knowledge comes from immersing oneself in the routines and customs that create a community.

Unveiling Traditions:
The town came alive with vivid music and dancing one evening as the community gathered for a cultural event. I wasn't simply a bystander; I was encouraged to participate
in the celebrations, learning the dance movements and rhythms with significant cultural meaning. I felt a strong connection to their history and a shared celebration of life as I swayed to the music with my newfound companions.

A Heartfelt Goodbye:
As my stay in the village drew to a close, I realized how valuable the relationships I had made with my host family and the community were. The departure was heartfelt, full of thanks and vows to keep in contact. The event broadened my horizons, challenged my ideas, and left an unforgettable imprint on my heart.

Participating in cultural exchanges and homestays in Zanzibar enabled me to bridge the gap between being a guest and being a part of the local fabric. Through shared experiences, shared tales, and shared laughs, I realized that true cultural immersion is about building genuine relationships that transcend boundaries and improve the human experience.

Preserving Tanzanian Heritage: A Responsible Tourism Path

A shared duty lies at the core of Tanzania's natural beauty and cultural treasures: the preservation of its rich history. Responsible tourism practices provide a guiding light, ensuring that the beauty and originality of this wonderful country be preserved for future generations.

Cultural Sensitivity and Respect:
As tourists, we have the opportunity to visit other communities and learn about their cultures. Cultural encounters must be approached with respect, openness, and a desire to learn. Participating in traditional practices, rituals, and socializing with locals should be led by sensitivity, to increase mutual understanding rather than disturb cultural norms.

Environmental Protection:
Tanzania's magnificent landscapes are awe-inspiring, but they are also fragile ecosystems that must be protected. Following designated paths, protecting animal habitats, and disposing of rubbish respectfully are all examples of responsible tourism. Choosing eco-friendly lodging and supporting conservation activities help to preserve these natural beauties.

Practical Participation:
Responsible tourism entails giving back in meaningful ways while connecting with local people and cultural places. Supporting local craftsmen, buying directly from them, and investing in community-driven initiatives empowers individuals while also providing long-term economic advantages. Participating in cultural exchanges and seminars not only broadens our horizons but also helps to preserve ancient crafts.

Communities Empowered:
The well-being of local communities is prioritized in responsible tourism activities. Choosing community-friendly lodgings, such as homestays and locally owned lodges, ensures that economic advantages are dispersed evenly. Participating in community-driven activities, such as schools or

health programs, benefits Tanzanian inhabitants in general.

Heritage Protection:
Historical monuments and landmarks must be preserved if Tanzania's cultural identity is to be preserved. Adhering to preservation criteria, obeying signs, and avoiding invasive behaviors all contribute to the preservation of these assets. Supporting cultural preservation initiatives and paying admission fees directly contributes to their upkeep.

Exchange of Culture, Not Exploitation:
Tanzanian culture is not a commodity to be exploited. Genuine cultural interchange is emphasized in responsible tourism, building ties that promote mutual respect and understanding. Conversations, exchanging experiences, and respecting the wisdom of local guides all contribute to meaningful interactions that benefit both passengers and hosts.

Education and Public Awareness:
Individual activities do not constitute responsible tourism. It entails teaching other tourists and creating awareness about environmentally friendly behaviors. We become positive change

ambassadors by advocating for responsible tourism, motivating people to approach their journeys with awareness, and a dedication to conserving Tanzania's history.

Preserving Tanzanian history via responsible tourism practices is a collaborative effort with the potential to protect the country's natural beauty and cultural diversity. By adhering to these values, we go on a trip that not only satisfies our travel dreams but also has a positive and long-lasting influence on the areas we visit, guaranteeing that future generations may enjoy Tanzania's grandeur in all its authenticity.

CHAPTER 7: Things to Do: Exciting Adventures for All Explorers

Tanzania has adventure at every turn, with a variety of activities to suit every sort of adventurer. There's something for everyone, whether you're a nature lover, a thrill seeker, or someone looking for cultural immersion.

Safari Glasses:
Take a safari to see the magnificence of Tanzania's animals up close. Awe-inspiring images of animals in their natural habitats may be seen in national parks such as the Serengeti and Ngorongoro Crater. Each moment is a portrait of nature in its purest form, from lions stalking the meadows to elephants roaming the savannah.

Summit Victories:
Mount Kilimanjaro is a dream come true for those looking for a challenge. You'll make your way to the peak, where the world spreads out under your feet, by trekking through varied ecosystems and weathering shifting sceneries. It's a victory of endurance and perseverance that rewards you with amazing vistas.

Seaside Happiness:
Zanzibar's beautiful sand beaches and blue seas entice visitors. The shore is a playground for aquatic experiences, whether you're sunbathing, swimming, or participating in exhilarating water sports like snorkeling and diving. Explore coral reefs teeming with life under the surface and discover colorful aquatic life.

Cultural Jewels:
Visit rural villages and marketplaces to immerse yourself in Tanzanian culture. Participate in traditional festivities, learn the technique of creating, and exchange tales with friendly people. Dance to traditional music and experience the aromas of real food to create memories that span cultures.

Historical Detours:
Discover the historical treasures of Zanzibar's Stone Town, where tiny streets and antique structures tell the story of the past. Wander around the busy bazaars, see ancient sites, and learn about the island's complex history. Every turn reveals a piece of the island's history waiting to be discovered.

Aerial Activities:
Take to the sky in a hot air balloon to see the Serengeti's enormous vistas from a different angle. Drift over herds of animals, catch the dawn across the horizon, and create images that highlight Tanzania's primal beauty.

Tanzania's abundance of activities assures that every adventurer's heart's content. This nation of marvels provides a diversity of experiences that will leave you with memories to enjoy for a lifetime, whether you're looking for heart-pounding thrills, tranquil natural beauty, or profound cultural connections.

Wildlife Safaris: Go on an Exciting Animal Adventure

Imagine exploring the heart of Tanzania's bush, where nature's rhythm sets the tone for an amazing safari. A wildlife tour takes you to a world where lions roam, elephants roar, and zebras graze freely. It's an exciting chance to see some of the world's most magnificent wildlife in their native environments.

The Five Greatest Challenges:
The thrill of seeing the Big Five — lions, elephants, buffalos, leopards, and rhinos – kicks off your safari trip. These famous beasts are the show's headliners, each embodying the pinnacle of Africa's wild beauty. You'll go on game drives with professional guides, examining the landscapes for telltale indications and spectacular encounters.

In addition to the Big Five:
While the Big Five takes center stage, Tanzania's environment is home to a diverse range of fascinating animals. Giraffes seek foliage with their long necks, cheetahs speed over the grassland, and playful hippos wallow in waterholes. Your safari adventure reveals a kaleidoscope of animals, with each species adding to the vivid fabric of the environment.

Different Habitats:
Tanzania's national parks and conservation zones provide a diverse range of habitats for the country's diverse wildlife. From the vast plains of the Serengeti, where the Great Migration takes place, to the lush vegetation of Ngorongoro Crater, each site provides a unique perspective on animal life. Because of the variety of sceneries, every moment is a discovery.

Professional Guidance:
On this wildlife adventure, guides are your friends and specialists. They watch animal movements, present interesting data, and provide insights into the habits of the species you meet using their excellent eyes and broad expertise. Each safari drive is transformed into an instructive and engaging experience thanks to their skills.

Silver Hours:
Wildlife excursions are magical during the golden hours of dawn and evening. Safaris at sunrise and dusk reveal a landscape painted in warm colors, when animals are most active. As you go off, the air is thick with expectancy, and the excitement of seeing elusive predators or watching a herd of elephants at play is an experience that will stay with you.

A wildlife safari in Tanzania is an enthralling experience that immerses you in the raw splendor of the animal realm. It's an opportunity to see the cycle of life, the delicate balance of ecosystems, and the majestic presence of species that have wandered these areas for generations. Every glimpse, every rustling in the grass, and every roar in the distance forms a symphony of nature that catches your heart and awakens your feeling of amazement as you travel through the woods.

Beyond Kilimanjaro Trekking & Hiking: Exploring Tanzania's Majestic Trails

While Mount Kilimanjaro is a well-known trekking destination, Tanzania has a wealth of other magnificent paths that promise stunning vistas, cultural contacts, and rewarding experiences. Beyond Kilimanjaro, you'll explore the varied and stunning paths that this lovely nation has to offer.

Ngorongoro Crater:
The Ngorongoro Conservation Area is a natural wonderland, and its highlands provide hikers with the opportunity to explore lush woods, undulating hills, and traditional Maasai towns. Trekking through this area shows spectacular landscapes as well as a chance to learn about the Maasai way of life, all while being surrounded by the natural beauty of the highlands.

Mountains of Usambara:
The Usambara Mountains are a hidden treasure, with lush slopes and charming settlements. Trekking across these mountains takes you down meandering roads that offer panoramic vistas,

terraced farmlands, and bustling local markets. It's an opportunity to immerse yourself in rural Tanzanian life and see how people and the environment coexist.

Mahale Mountain Range:
The Mahale Mountains appeal with their distant and unspoiled beauty for a one-of-a-kind hiking adventure. This is where chimps walk freely, and hikers may see these amazing animals in their natural environment. The trip is about more than simply the goal; it's about the beautiful animals and the feeling of adventure that comes with venturing into the unknown.

Camel Safari in Mkuru:
Consider a camel safari through the Mkuru Camel Camp in Northern Tanzania for a unique trip. This eco-friendly adventure takes you on a cultural and aesthetic experience, enabling you to travel the regions with these gentle giants. It's a fusion of traditional and contemporary, providing a unique viewpoint on Tanzania's beauty.

Lake Natron Expedition:
The strange landscapes that surround Lake Natron are a geological treasure trove. Trekking here reveals salt flats, old lava flows, and the chance to

see the vivid colors of flamingos gathered along the shoreline. It's a journey into an exceptional area that few people get to see.

Beyond Kilimanjaro, trekking and climbing invite you to explore Tanzania's various and interesting terrains. Each route provides a unique viewpoint, a fresh cultural experience, and an opportunity to interact with nature in its purest form. Tanzania's trails offer an incredible trip that will leave you with memories carved in your heart and a better respect for the country's rich and diverse landscapes, whether you're heading into highlands, mountains, or distinct ecosystems.

Uncovering Tanzania's Hidden Caves and Grottos

Tanzania's surface hides a world of secrets waiting to be discovered - a kingdom of subterranean treasures beckoning the daring visitor. From complex tunnels covered with sparkling formations to awe-inspiring grottos, these underground landscapes provide a one-of-a-kind and enthralling journey.

The Caves of Chinhoyi:
The Chinhoyi Caves are a stunning network of limestone tunnels and emerald-blue ponds located in Zimbabwe, within a stone's throw from Tanzania. Descending into the depths exposes a bizarre world of stalactites and stalagmites, as well as crystal-clear water. The "Sleeping Pool," the major attraction, is a marvel to behold: an underground lake with water so transparent that you can see the cavern walls below.

The Amboni Caves:
Travel to Tanga, Tanzania's coastline area, and you'll come across the Amboni Caves, a complex of interconnecting chambers with geological marvels and historical value. You'll be met with fascinating rock formations, ancient inscriptions, and a feeling of wonder that comes with unraveling the tales buried below the ground as you explore the labyrinthine pathways.

The Caves of Korogwe:
The Korogwe Caves, with its captivating stalactites and stalagmites that create otherworldly creations, are a tribute to nature's ingenuity. These caverns, located in the Lushoto area, are not only a geological wonder but also have cultural significance for the local tribes. Exploring their

depths reveals the forces that have sculpted the globe over millions of years.

Zanzibar Grottos:
Tumbatu, an island off the coast of Zanzibar, is home to exquisite grottos that urge you to enter a secret paradise. With towering chambers, azure seas, and ethereal light seeping through breaches in the rock, these sea caves are nature's cathedrals. Exploring these grottos takes you to a realm where time appears to have stopped.

Unknown Depths:
Exploring Tanzania's caverns and grottos is more than simply a physical excursion; it's about digging into the earth's past and discovering the mysteries that lie underneath. Each cave tells a tale of geological development and human interaction, providing a look into the past as well as the feeling of awe that comes with exploring the unknown.

Tanzania's subterranean treasures are proof of the earth's complex beauty and the delights that await those who explore under the surface. Delving into these underground environments gives a unique viewpoint that deepens your awareness of the world's hidden treasures, from magnificent formations to the sensation of wonder that comes with discovery.

Zanzibar's Relaxation and Wellness Oasis

A sanctuary of tranquility awaits visitors seeking restoration of mind, body, and spirit in the middle of Zanzibar's dynamic energy and stunning surroundings. The island's magnificent spas and tranquil retreats provide a haven where relaxation reigns supreme and wellness is elevated to an art form.

Beachside Happiness:
Imagine the soft sound of waves lulling you into a state of happiness as you indulge in a seaside spa experience, where the rhythmic ebb and flow of the ocean lulls you into a state of ecstasy. Beachfront spas in Zanzibar provide an exquisite environment for treatments inspired by both traditional and contemporary therapeutic methods. Each treatment, from reviving massages to energizing body washes, is a beautiful ballet of indulgence and regeneration.

Healing Retreats:
Wellness retreats in Zanzibar are a place for individuals seeking holistic healing and calm introspection. These resorts, nestled among lush gardens or situated on clifftops overlooking the Indian Ocean, provide a comprehensive approach to well-being. Yoga sessions, meditation courses, and health seminars serve as the foundation of these transforming experiences, taking you on a path to inner balance and harmony.

Traditional Knowledge:
The rich cultural past of Zanzibar is incorporated into its health offers. Many spas use locally derived materials as well as traditional methods in their treatments. Experience the soothing touch of local therapists, who rely on decades of experience to give treatments that nourish the body and boost the soul. Traditional therapies, such as the Zanzibar spice massage, attest to the island's close relationship with nature and plenty of resources.

Nature Reserves:
The natural beauty of Zanzibar extends to its spa retreats, where lush gardens and tranquil surroundings create a scene for relaxation. Some spas are hidden away in private villas, enabling you to enjoy specialized treatments in the comfort of

your own home. These natural oases allow you to rest in nature's embrace, whether it's a massage under the shadow of swaying palms or a plunge in a calm pool.

Sense Rejuvenation:
Spas in Zanzibar engage all of the senses in a symphony of relaxation, from scented essential oils to therapeutic rituals. The aromas of local spices, the calming sounds of ocean waves, and the soft touch of professional therapists transport you to a state of complete relaxation. Every treatment is a journey to rejuvenation that will leave you feeling refreshed and energized.

Spas and retreats in Zanzibar provide more than simply enjoyment; they invite you to reconnect with yourself and find peace in the embrace of tranquillity. These havens of leisure and health, nestled within the island's rich culture and breathtaking scenery, enable you to go on a journey of self-care and change, leaving you rejuvenated and ready to tackle the world afresh.

Zanzibar's Environmental Commitment: Eco-Tourism and Conservation Initiatives

A healthy collaboration between tourism and conservation is taking root in Zanzibar, the gem of the Indian Ocean, opening the path for a sustainable future that appreciates both the beauty of the island and its sensitive ecosystems. Zanzibar is preserving its natural assets for future generations via eco-tourism and careful conservation programs.

Maintaining Marine Diversity:
The crystal-clear seas and vivid coral reefs of Zanzibar are home to a plethora of marine life. Ecotourism in this area lays a significant focus on ethical snorkeling and diving activities, ensuring that these fragile ecosystems are not damaged. Dive operators and guides follow stringent standards of behavior, teaching guests the value of protecting marine life and reef integrity.

Conservation of Sea Turtles:
The beaches of Zanzibar serve as breeding places for endangered sea turtles. Conservation efforts monitor nesting locations, relocate eggs to secure hatcheries, and raise awareness about the need for

sea turtle conservation. Visitors may see hatchlings being released into the water, which aids in the preservation of these ancient sailors.
Responsible Accommodations:
Zanzibar's eco-friendly villas and resorts are setting the standard for sustainable hospitality. These lodgings focus on reducing their ecological imprint, from solar-powered energy systems to water conservation methods. Guests may practice responsible tourism by staying in eco-friendly accommodations that reflect their beliefs.

Initiatives Led by the Community:
Zanzibar's conservation efforts extend beyond its natural settings. Community-led programs enable residents to have an active part in environmental preservation. Residents are pushing good change and contributing to the island's general well-being via programs like trash management, reforestation, and sustainable agriculture.

Educational Background:
In Zanzibar, ecotourism is also about educating and raising awareness. Visitors may take guided nature walks, where trained guides give information about the island's flora, animals, and conservation initiatives. These encounters not only broaden

comprehension but also develop a bond between visitors and the environment.

Cultural Protection:
The cultural legacy of Zanzibar is intertwined with its natural beauty. Conservation efforts assist local populations in conserving traditional activities ranging from handicrafts to agricultural methods. Visitors who interact with these cultural assets help to preserve Zanzibar's distinctive character and legacy.

Zanzibar's dedication to eco-tourism and conservation projects exemplifies a balanced approach to travel, one that appreciates the island's stunning scenery while also protecting its vulnerable ecosystems and empowering local populations. Visitors who embrace responsible tourism and support these projects become environmental stewards and collaborators in ensuring that Zanzibar's natural and cultural treasures thrive for future generations.

Chapter 8: Resources and Practical Information for Your Zanzibar Adventure

A trip to Zanzibar requires careful preparation and a lot of relevant information to guarantee a pleasant and pleasurable experience. Here's a complete reference to practical tools that help improve your Zanzibar vacation, whether you're planning your trip, navigating the island's attractions, or seeking assistance during your stay.

Essentials for Travel:
Visa Requirements: Determine if you need a visa to enter Tanzania or Zanzibar. Before your journey, get the appropriate visa.
Health Precautions: Before flying, consult a travel clinic for required immunizations and health precautions.

Navigating and Exchanging Currency in Zanzibar

Understanding the local currency and how to conduct money conversion is critical for a pleasant and trouble-free trip to Zanzibar. Here's a complete guide on navigating the island's currency:

Currency:
The Tanzanian Shilling (TZS) is the official currency of both Zanzibar and Tanzania. It is denoted by the symbols "TSh" or "TZS."

Money Denominations:
Tanzanian Shilling is available in both coins and banknotes. The most common coin denominations are 50, 100, and 200 shillings. Banknotes come in a variety of denominations, including 500, 1000, 5000, 10,000, and 20,000 shillings.

Exchange Rates:
Major airports, banks, authorized exchange offices, and certain hotels provide currency exchange services. To guarantee fair prices and prevent fraud, it is best to convert money at authorized exchange locations. Although hotels and resorts may provide currency exchange services, the prices may be less beneficial.

ATMs:
ATMs (Automated Teller Machines) are common in metropolitan locations, including Stone Town and important tourist destinations. They accept major credit and debit cards from across the world. Remember that certain smaller cities and rural

locations may have restricted ATM availability, so withdraw cash before going into distant places.

Foreign Exchange Rates:
Exchange rates often fluctuate, so it's best to compare prices at different exchange sites before completing a purchase. You may approximate the current exchange rate by using currency conversion applications or websites.

Cash or Credit Card:
While credit and debit cards are accepted at certain hotels, restaurants, and stores in cities, it is best to have some local currency in cash on hand for minor purchases, transit, and markets. Card acceptance may be restricted in rural and distant places.

Currency Guidelines:
Bringing foreign cash into Tanzania or Zanzibar is not restricted. However, any sum above USD 10,000 must be declared upon admission.

Currency Advice:
- Inform your bank of your trip dates and destination to prevent problems with credit card transactions.
- Keep some local cash on hand for little transactions and transportation.

- Use caution while handling cash and avoid flaunting huge sums in public.

Considerations for COVID-19:
Because of the continuing epidemic, it is best to avoid personal touch by using contactless payment options wherever feasible. Additionally, look for any revised COVID-19 instructions or changes in currency conversion processes.

You'll be better able to handle your funds and make the most of your stay on this lovely island if you're acquainted with Zanzibar's currency and currency exchange procedures.

Language & Phrases for Getting Around Zanzibar

While English is frequently spoken and understood in Zanzibar, learning a few basic Swahili words can enrich your experience
and allow you to interact with the local culture. Here are some terms to help you travel to Zanzibar easily:

Greetings:
- Good day, Jambo.
- Good day: Habari ya asubuhi

- Good day: Habari ya mchana
- Hello and good evening: Habari ya Jori
- How are you doing?: Gani, habari?
Nzuri: I'm alright.

Initial Phrases:
- Ndiyo, yes.
No, Hapana.
- Tafadhali, please.
- Regards, Asante
- Thank you very much: Karibu
- Please excuse me / Please accept my apologies: Samahani
- Farewell: Kwaheri

How to Get Around:
- Can you tell me where...?: Wapi iko...?
- How much does this cost?: Hello, ni bei gani?
- I'd want to visit...: Nataka kwenda...
- Kushoto (left)
- On the right: Kulia
- To the right: Moja kwa moja

Dining and Food:
- Maji (water)
- Cuisine: Chakula
- Kifungua kinywa for breakfast
- Chakula cha mchana for lunch

- Chakula cha jioni for dinner
- Delectable: Kitamu

Numbers:
- Number one: Moja
- Number two: Mbili
- Number three: Tatu
- Number four: Nne
Tano is number five.
- Number ten: Kumi

Emergencies:
- Help!: Hello, Saidia!
- I need the services of a doctor: Nahitaji Daktari
- Polisi: police
- Hospital

Shopping:
- What is the price of this?: Hello, ni bei gani?
- Could you please offer me a discount?: Kunipunguzia unaweza bei?
- I'd want to have...: Ningependa...

Cultural Manners:
- Be respectful of local traditions and dress modestly, particularly while visiting religious sites or communities.

- Always get permission before photographing individuals.
- Smile and greet them with a cheerful "Jambo" or "Habari."

Exploring and Participating:
- Could you tell me your name?: Nani, jina lako?
- Hello, my name is...: Jina langu ni...
- Where do you come from?: Wapi unatoka?
- It's a pleasure to meet you: Nafurahi kukuona

Date and Time:
- Can you tell me what time it is?: What is your name?
- Today is Leo's birthday.
- Kesho will be held tomorrow.
- Climate: Hali ya hewa

Considerations for COVID-19:
- Barakoa face mask
- Social segregation: Umbali wa kijamii
- Sanitizer for hands: Dawa ya kusafishia mikono

Learning and utilizing a few Swahili words not only allows you to speak more successfully but also demonstrates your respect and enthusiasm for the local culture. Even a simple "Jambo" or "Asante" might help you make important relationships throughout your stay in Zanzibar.

Transportation Options and Costs to Zanzibar and Kilimanjaro

Traveling to Zanzibar and Kilimanjaro requires a range of transportation alternatives, each of which provides a distinct experience. Here's a breakdown of how to get to these locations, along with projected costs:

How to Get to Zanzibar:
1. **Flights:** The most frequent method to get to Zanzibar is to fly into Stone Town's Abeid Amani Karume International Airport (ZNZ). Several international and regional airlines fly to Zanzibar. Flight prices might vary depending on variables such as departure location, travel dates, and prior booking. Prices for round-trip flights from major cities to Zanzibar normally range between $400 and USD 800.

2. **Ferries:** Ferries connect Dar es Salaam (Tanzania's capital) to Zanzibar. The boat voyage provides a gorgeous path and is a less expensive choice than flying. Prices vary depending on the class and operator. Make sure to reserve your

tickets ahead of time, particularly during busy tourist seasons.

How to Get to Kilimanjaro:
1. **Flights:** Kilimanjaro International Airport (JRO) is the primary entry point into the Kilimanjaro area. Many international airlines fly to JRO from cities all around the globe. Flight prices are determined by variables such as departure location, travel dates, and booking time.

2. **Local Flights:** If you are already in Tanzania, you may take a local flight to Kilimanjaro International Airport (JRO) from Julius Nyerere International Airport (DAR) in Dar es Salaam or other major airports. Prices for domestic flights might vary.

3. **Overland Travel:** If you're already in Tanzania, you may take a bus or a private car to Kilimanjaro. The road trip provides an opportunity to enjoy the country's landscapes, but it is necessary to prepare for lengthier travel durations.

Cost Factors to Consider:
- Flight prices vary greatly based on a variety of parameters such as departure location, airline selection, booking time, and travel season.

Round-trip flight prices may vary from a few hundred dollars to over a thousand dollars.
- Ferry prices between Dar es Salaam and Zanzibar vary according to class (economy, business, and so on) and operator. Prices are often lower when compared to flights.
- Domestic flights inside Tanzania may vary in price depending on the route and carrier.
- The cost of overland travel is determined by the form of transportation (bus, private car, etc.), the route, and the distance.

Local Public Transportation:

- **Taxis:** Taxis are a widely used means of transportation. Negotiate rates ahead of time or use metered taxis.
- **Dala-Dalas:** For short journeys, shared minivans are a cost-effective solution.

Considerations for COVID-19:
Before arranging your trip, be sure to check for any COVID-19-related travel restrictions, entrance procedures, and health standards. These regulations might affect travel logistics and expenses.

Note: Prices and availability are subject to change, so it is best to check current pricing and possibilities closer to your trip dates. Additionally, for the most up-to-date information, contact travel companies, airlines, or transportation providers.

Accommodation:
- ****Zanzibar Accommodation Options: Types, Locations, and Cost**

Zanzibar has a wide choice of hotel alternatives to suit all budgets and interests. You'll find a location to stay that meets your requirements, from luxurious resorts to small guesthouses. Here's an overview of different kinds of lodging, popular places, and projected costs:

**1. **Leisure Resorts and Boutique Hotels:
- **Destinations:** Nungwi, Kendwa, Michamvi, Paje, Matemwe, and Stone Town
- **Description:** Zanzibar is home to several high-end beachfront resorts and boutique hotels that provide lavish facilities, private beaches, spa services, and delectable eating choices.
- **Estimated Price:** Prices vary greatly depending on the resort, hotel type, and season. Luxury resorts and boutique hotels may cost

anything from $300 to USD 1,000 per night or more.

2. Hotels and lodges in the middle price range:
- **Locations:** Stone Town, Jambiani, Kiwengwa, Nungwi, Paje, and others
- **Description:** Mid-priced hotels and lodges provide decent lodgings as well as facilities like pools, restaurants, and convenient access to the beach. They strike a decent mix between quality and price.
- **Estimated Price:** Prices for mid-range alternatives may vary from $100 and $300 USD each night.

3. Guesthouses and Hostels on a Budget:
- **Destinations:** Stone Town, Nungwi, Paje, and Jambiani
- **Description:** Low-cost guesthouses and hostels are ideal for tourists looking for a basic and inexpensive place to stay. These motels often provide modest conveniences, common places, and the opportunity to meet other visitors.
- **Estimated Cost:** Depending on the location and amenities, budget guesthouses and hostels may range from $20 to USD 50 per night.

**4. **Airbnb and Vacation Rentals
- **places:** Zanzibar's various places
- **Description:** Airbnb and vacation rentals allow you to stay in various lodgings including seaside cottages, flats, and traditional Swahili homes.
- **Estimated Cost:** Prices range from $50 to USD 200 a night or more depending on the kind of rental and location.

5. Environmentally Friendly Lodges & Retreats:
- **Places:** Jambiani, Paje, Michamvi
- **Description:** Eco-friendly resorts and retreats in Zanzibar promote sustainability and eco-conscious methods. These lodgings often emphasize nature, health, and local culture.
- **Estimated Price:** Although prices vary, eco-friendly resorts and retreats typically range from $100 to USD 300 per night.

Cost Factors to Consider:
- The cost of lodging may vary greatly depending on criteria such as location, hotel type, facilities, and season.
- Peak tourist seasons, such as December to January and June to August, tend to have higher prices.

Booking Suggestion:
- It's best to book your lodgings ahead of time, particularly if you're going during peak season, to secure your favorite accommodation and maybe obtain cheaper pricing.

Please keep in mind that the anticipated expenses are based on general trends and may vary. It is best to study individual lodgings, check online booking platforms, and contact the establishments directly for the most accurate and up-to-date information.

- Cultural Manners:
- **Respect:** Respect local norms, dress modestly in public, and get permission before photographing individuals.
- **Tipping:** Tipping is typically accepted, particularly for excellent service at restaurants, hotels, and tour guides.

- Tours and Activities:
- **Tour companies:** For excursions, safaris, and aquatic sports, choose renowned tour companies. Read reviews and weigh your alternatives.
- **Activity Reservations:** To guarantee your space, book popular activities like diving, snorkeling, and wildlife excursions in advance.

- Health and security:
- **Travel Insurance:** Purchase comprehensive travel insurance that includes coverage for medical emergencies and trip cancellations.
- **Health Facilities:** Learn about area medical facilities and contact information in case of an emergency.

- Local Laws and Customs:
- **Drug Laws:** Possession of illicit substances is forbidden and punishable by harsh penalties.
- **Cultural Sensitivity:** When visiting local communities and religious places, dress modestly.

- Climate and Clothing:
- **Climate:** The island of Zanzibar has a tropical climate. Pack light clothes, comfy shoes, and a swimsuit.
- **Wet Season:** April to May and November to December are the wet seasons. If you are going during these times, bring rain gear.

- Neighborhood Resources:
- **Tourist Information Centers:** Stop by your local tourist information center for maps, brochures, and help.
- **Local Guides:** Use local guides to learn about local culture and history.

Considerations for COVID-19:
- **Travel limitations:** Before your journey, check for any COVID-19-related travel limitations or regulations.
- **Health Protocols:** Adhere to health protocols, wear masks in public, and follow social distancing rules.

Zanzibar Emergency Contacts: Be Prepared and Stay Safe

When visiting Zanzibar, it is essential to have access to emergency contacts in case you need help. Here are some crucial phone numbers and contacts to have on hand throughout your stay:

Police, Fire, and Medical Calls:
Call 911 for a police emergency
- 115 for Medical Emergencies
- 114th Fire Department

Hospitals and Medical Centers:
+255 24 2232255 Mnazi Mmoja Hospital (Stone Town)
+255 22 2151000 Muhimbili National Hospital (Dar es Salaam)

- +255 22 2115151 Aga Khan Hospital (Dar es Salaam)

Consulates and Embassies:
If you are a foreign citizen, it is a good idea to be aware of your country's embassy or consulate in Tanzania or Zanzibar. They may help with emergencies, missing passports, and other consular problems.

COVID-19 Support Line:
- Information Hotline for COVID-19: 199
Please keep in mind that this information is subject to change as the situation evolves.

Local Tour Operators and Hotels:
It's also a good idea to retain the contact information for your local tour operator and your hotel's front desk on hand. If you run into any problems during your journey, they may give advice and support.

- Communication Suggestions:
- Check that your phone is charged and has credit or data.
- If you have a local SIM card, keep vital phone numbers on it.

- When checking into a hotel, ask the front desk for local emergency contact information.
- **Mobile Networks:** Local mobile network SIM cards may be purchased. Examine the statistics and call rates.
- **Internet:** Wi-Fi is provided in many hotels and public spaces.

- Personal Safety Recommendations:
- Keep a copy of your passport, travel insurance, and vital papers in a safe place at all times.
- Tell someone you trust about your intentions to go and share your itinerary with them.
- Before your vacation, get acquainted with local cultures, laws, and safety precautions.

Having access to emergency contacts and being prepared for unexpected scenarios may help you have a safe and happy vacation in Zanzibar.

Your Zanzibar journey will undoubtedly be memorable and enlightening. You'll be well-prepared to explore the island, immerse yourself in its delights, and create memorable experiences that will remain with you long after your visit is over if you arm yourself with practical knowledge and resources.

CHAPTER 9- Conclusion: Embrace Zanzibar's Jewel and Conquer Kilimanjaro's Summit

As your adventure through the picturesque paradise of Zanzibar and ascent to the magnificent heights of Kilimanjaro concludes, you will depart with memories seared in your heart and a feeling of awe that only nature's beauties can evoke. Zanzibar's beautiful beaches, colorful culture, and rich history greeted you warmly, while Kilimanjaro's towering presence stretched your boundaries and rewarded you with stunning views. Your voyage has been a tapestry of wonderful moments, from the sunsets over the Indian Ocean to the victorious moment atop Africa's highest mountain.

Your discovery of Zanzibar's hidden jewels, interactions with residents, and immersion in Tanzanian life has provided you with a better knowledge of this wonderful corner of the globe. You've explored the heart and soul of these places via cultural exchanges, animal safaris, and off-the-beaten-path excursions, establishing ties that transcend boundaries.

As you reflect on your adventure, keep in mind that the memories you've made and the lessons you've learned are the genuine riches you'll bring back with you. These moments, whether walking along Zanzibar's beautiful beaches, marveling at its marine life, or staring at the stars from the peak of Kilimanjaro, are testaments to the irrepressible spirit of discovery that dwells inside all of us.

Zanzibar and Kilimanjaro have disclosed their secrets to you, and you now keep them near to your heart, eternally woven into the fabric of your tale. May the spirit of Zanzibar's beaches and Kilimanjaro's peaks guide, inspire, and remind you of the endless beauty and opportunity that await you as you continue to travel the globe and start on new adventures.

Farewell, traveler, but know that the memories you've made will be with you for the rest of your life. Until the next adventure beckons, may the romance of Zanzibar and the victory of Kilimanjaro's summit live on in your heart.

Looking Back on Your Zanzibar and Kilimanjaro Adventures

A tapestry of unique memories develops before you as you reflect on your incredible adventure across the enchanting landscapes of Zanzibar and the awe-inspiring heights of Kilimanjaro. Your journey has been a symphony of discovery, culture, and nature's majesty, from the beautiful beaches of Zanzibar's coast to the victorious top of Africa's highest mountain.

Zanzibar greeted you with its emerald seas, colorful culture, and historical allure. The secret treasures you discovered, as well as the warm welcome of local communities, have left an unforgettable impact on your heart. The frenetic dance of life in Zanzibar's streets, the vivid traditions, and the calming tranquility of its beaches have all become part of your own tale.

Then came Kilimanjaro, a massive challenge and unrivaled achievement. With each step closer to the peak, you learned the strength of resolve and the tenacity of the human spirit. The stunning vistas, different ecosystems, and companionship of other trekkers are memories that will inspire and elevate you for the rest of your life.

As you reflect on your voyage, keep in mind that the memories you've made are a monument to your bravery, curiosity, and desire to embrace the unknown. The things you save are the sunsets, starry evenings, laughter shared with locals, and victorious moments at the summit.

Your trip to Zanzibar and Kilimanjaro has enhanced your soul, enlarged your perspectives, and given you a great feeling of connectedness to the world around you. As you continue on your journey, may the beauty of Zanzibar and the grandeur of Kilimanjaro guide and inspire you in all your future experiences.

Making Long-Lasting Memories

The moments you gather become the threads that weave together the tale of your voyage in the tapestry of your travels. Remember that the actual riches you carry are the memories you build along the way as you discover the breathtaking landscapes of Zanzibar and scale the magnificent heights of Kilimanjaro.

Every stride on Zanzibar's beautiful beaches, every touching connection with local people, and every stunning vista from Kilimanjaro's top are imprinted on your heart and soul. These are the keepsakes that transcend the physical, reminding you of the world's beauty, resilience, and amazement.

Capture the laughter shared with new companions, the awe-inspiring gasps at nature's magnificence, and the calm moments of introspection as you soak in the spirit of your surroundings. These are the ethereal mementos that no trinket can replace, the timeless photographs that time cannot erase.

Allow these memories to be your guiding lights as you go ahead. Allow them to inspire, motivate, and remind you of the endless possibilities that await you in every part of the world. Cherish the moments since they are the real keepsakes of your Zanzibar and Kilimanjaro voyage, permanently creating a tapestry of beauty, exploration, and unforgettable encounters.

My Memorable Travel Experience

Once upon a time, I set off on an exciting voyage to a faraway region known as Zanzibar. I felt the warm embrace of the sun and the soothing caress of the ocean wind the instant I stepped foot on its beautiful sandy beaches. The crystal-clear seas danced before my eyes as I wandered down the shore, enticing me to take a bath in their soothing embrace.

Exploring Zanzibar's rich culture was like walking into a live picture. I strolled through Stone Town's lovely alleys, where history echoed through historic buildings and small lanes. The vibrant marketplaces were a rainbow of colors and fragrances, with each corner conveying a different tale about the island's history and present.

But the true adventure was still to come: the iconic Kilimanjaro climb. I found new levels of power and drive inside myself with each step up the mountain's high slopes. As I ascended higher, the environment changed from lush woods to bizarre alpine deserts. And then came the moment when I stood atop Africa's roof, staring out at a universe of clouds under my feet.

But it wasn't simply the stunning sights that stayed with me. Friendships built along the journey shared laughter and tales passed over campfires, and victorious celebrations at the peak will live on in my memories.

As I think about my voyage, I'm reminded that travel is about connecting with the globe and other travelers, not simply exploring new locations. Whether you're sunbathing on the beaches of Zanzibar or scaling the peaks of Kilimanjaro, the tales we create and share are the threads that connect us all in a tapestry of travel and discovery. So here's to the great memories, newfound friends, and unlimited opportunities that lie ahead. Wishing you safe travels, my fellow travelers!

Inspiring future trips and adventures

A universe of possibilities opens up before you as you think about your adventure through the breathtaking landscapes of Zanzibar and your heroic summit of Kilimanjaro. The memories you've made and the experiences you've had are just a taste of the adventures that lie ahead.

Imagine roaming through lively marketplaces in other locations, eating unusual delicacies that tickle your taste buds, and connecting with people from various cultures. Imagine yourself standing atop unknown peaks, seeing stunning sunsets over unexplored vistas, and immersing yourself in the splendor of our planet's natural beauties.

The spirit of inquiry and discovery that has led you on your voyage remains with you. Allow it to drive your ambitions and desires, creating a desire inside you to discover more, learn more, and connect more profoundly with the world around you.

Whether you're following in the footsteps of ancient civilizations, going on animal safaris in remote savannas, or taking daring hikes into untamed wilderness, the globe is your canvas, ready for you to paint it with your own unique experiences and tales.

So, let your heart be your guide and your curiosity be your compass. The route of future experiences is ahead of you, waiting to unveil its hidden gems and memorable moments. Embrace the uncertainty, love the adventure, and continue to create your life's tale with each step you take. The world is wide, and your next adventure awaits you with open arms. Here's to the boundless possibilities that await you - may your future travels be filled with wonder, discovery, and the delight of discovering new vistas.

Printed in Great Britain
by Amazon